101 Ways To Tie A Scarf

S. Denise Hoyle

Copyright © 1988-2017 S. Denise Hoyle

All rights reserved.

ISBN: 1544147503
ISBN-13: 978-1544147505

CONTENTS

1	How To Make Scarves	1
2	Flattering Your Figure	3
3	Head Wraps	5
4	Classic Head Wrap	6
5	Criss-Cross Head Wrap	8
6	Forehead Drape	10
7	Smooth Forehead Drape	11
8	The Side Rosette	12
9	Full Covering Side Rosette	14
10	The Hair Wrap	15
11	Classy Hair Cover	17
12	Everyday Hair Cover	19
13	Classy Everyday Hair Cover	20
14	Poor Weather Hideaway	22
15	Windy Day Cover-Up	24
16	Tri-Colored Hair Holder	26
17	Stylish Hair Holder	27
18	Neck Wraps	29

19	Rope Tie	30
20	Choker	31
21	Necklace	32
22	Bow Tie	33
23	Flower Tie	34
24	The Loose Ascot	35
25	The Romantic Twist	37
26	The Western Ascot	39
27	Unfinished Western Ascot	41
28	Formal Ascot	42
29	Finished Ascot	44
30	Rope Necklace	46
31	Neck Twist	47
32	Rope Twist	49
33	Neck Tie	51
34	Casual Rope	53
35	Neck Rosette	55
36	Loose Neck Bow	57
37	Shoulder Wrap	59
38	Side Wrap	61

39	Collar Dresser	62
40	Neck Wrap Knot	64
41	Pleated Flower Wrap	66
42	Casual Pleated Flower	68
43	Puffed Neck Wrap	69
44	Looped Neck Wrap	71
45	Pleated Neck Wrap	73
46	The Square Knot	75
47	Tailored Neck Tie	77
48	The Windsor Knot	78
49	Traditional Bow Tie	80
50	Basic Bows	82
51	Using A Buckle	84
52	Waist Wraps	85
53	Braided Waist Wrap	86
54	Sash	87
55	Knotted Waist Wrap	88
56	Flowered Waist Wrap	89
57	Looped Waist Wrap	90
58	Tops & Skirts	93

59	Hip Wrap & Bandeau	94
60	Halter Top	96
61	Blouson	98
62	Criss-Cross Halter	100
63	Slashed Bikini Top	101
64	Bodice	102
65	Bikini Top & Skirt	104
66	Shawls	107
67	Draped Shawl	108
68	Folded Shawl	110
69	Knotted Shawl	112
70	Hat Wraps	115
71	Ruffled Hat Wrap	116
72	Roped Hat Wrap	117
73	Bowed Hat Wrap	118
74	Pleated Hat Wrap	119
75	Using A Scarf Clip	121
76	Head Wrap	122
77	Full Head Wrap	124
78	Pirate's Cap	126

79	Bonnet	127
80	Bow Tie Head Wrap	129
81	Ruffled Flower	131
82	Bowed Head Wrap	133
83	Loose Hair Cover	135
84	Knotted Head Wrap	137
85	Neck Wrap	139
86	Choker	141
87	Half Bow	143
88	Neck Bow	145
89	Multi-Colored Neck Bow	146
90	Ruffled Neck Bow	148
91	Triangular Neck Wrap	150
92	Double Neck Panel	152
93	Shoulder Bow	153
94	Clipped Ascot	154
95	Puffed Ascot	156
96	Puffed Jabot	158
97	Bowed Ascot	160
98	Clipped Collar	162

99	Puffy Collar	164
100	Ruffled Collar	165
101	Bowed Collar	167
102	Flowered Collar	169
103	Puffed Flower	171
104	Side Clipped Wrap	173
105	Full Neck Wrap	174
106	Classy Neck Wrap	175
107	Clipped Romantic Twist	176
108	Heightening Neck Wrap	178
109	Conclusion	180
110	Resources	181

1 HOW TO MAKE SCARVES

The scarf can be the most stylish and adaptable accessory you own! Scarves can help you build a fashionable wardrobe without demolishing your budget. Creatively used, the scarf can provide many changes of look for your wardrobe and can even be used to flatter your figure or draw attention away from any figure faults you may have.

When fashioning your own scarves you must first decide on the size. Medium to large squares are the most versatile and are suitable as suit and blouse fillers, can substitute for a blouse, and are ideal for coats. Small squares are accent pieces only. Small squares measure less than 24 inches. Medium squares are from 24 to 27 inches. Large squares are 30 inches or more.

Oblong scarves are usually considered an accent item with the exception of wool scarves which are usually designed for warmth. The oblong scarf is an ideal accessory for suits, dresses, blouses and sweaters. For oblong scarves, a medium size would be approximately 11 by 54 inches. The sizes of oblong scarves may vary considerably.

Normally you would use silk for your dressy scarves, wool for warm scarves and the economical cotton mainly for head or neck covering, but you can use your imagination to come up with your own styles.

Some helpful hints when selecting your materials are to select patterns and textures that are compatible with the patterns and textures already in your wardrobe; wear or bring along a sample of the garment you will wear with your scarf; keep versatility in mind; experiment with color and select good quality material. Also, if you give yourself plenty of time when selecting your material, you will be generally happier with your decisions.

Now that you have decided on the size and material for your scarf, you need to decide on whether you want a fringe or a finished edge. If you decide on a fringe, remember to leave 2 to 3 extra inches of material on each side of your square. Sew your seam 2 to 3 inches from the edge of each side of your square and then unravel the edges.

You may want to tie off your fringe in small amounts all the way around your scarf for better staying power. If you decide on a finished edge, it should be rolled and well topstitched approximately 1/8" from the edge. To give your scarf that good quality look the edges should parallel exactly when the scarf is folded in half from any direction.

Handle your scarves with gentle care. Follow the fabric manufacturer's instructions when washing or cleaning your scarves or follow these guidelines. Acrylic materials should be hand washed. Polyester scarves can be hand or machine-washed. Silks should always be dry-cleaned. Wool should be dry-cleaned or hand washed. Always clean your scarves before they become too soiled, as this will extend the life of your scarves. Also, it may be a good idea to wash your material before cutting and sewing it in case of shrinkage, with the exception of silks, which should only be dry-cleaned.

Now that your scarf is finished, the next important step is learning how to fashion the scarf into one of numerous creative shapes and folds, which will add a touch of class to any outfit!

2 FLATTERING YOUR FIGURE

Scarves can be used in a variety of ways to help flatter your figure by accentuating attributes and/or hiding flaws! Use the following tips to enhance your bust line, slim full hips, hide a sagging neck or double chin, even add or subtract height!

Color can be used to either hide or accentuate. Use bright colors or patterns to draw attention to an area or use dark and/or monotone colors to hide flaws. For instance, you can fold a dark (black, navy, etc.) square scarf in half into a triangle and tie it around your middle with the knot on one side to de-emphasize a full waist or hips. Also, you can use a brightly colored scarf around your neck or waist to draw attention to the upper torso, and away from the lower body.

You can give the illusion of added height by tying a scarf in colors to match your outfit around your neck or head, or you can trail a long rectangular scarf over your shoulder for the same effect. Conversely, tying a scarf of a different color around your neck or head can have the effect of detracting from your height.

Any of the neck wrap styles may be used to hide a sagging neck or double chin. Some of the head wrap styles are also effective. Try the scarf clip styles for added interest.

Ascot styles, particularly using colorful or patterned scarves, can be used to accentuate the bust line. Scarf clips can also be used to draw attention to the area. Shawl styles or over the shoulder styles are useful when attempting to de-emphasize the chest area.

The main thing to remember when tying scarves is to be creative. Have fun trying as many styles as necessary until you find one that works with your outfit. Scarves are versatile accessories that have never gone out of style and you can use them to expand your wardrobe inexpensively.

3 HEAD WRAPS

Head wraps are perfect for windy days or for those "bad hair" days when you still want to look well put together.

5 CRISS-CROSS HEAD WRAP

Fold two oblong scarves in half lengthwise. Place one on top of the other to form a cross.

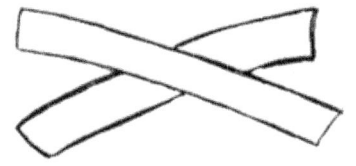

Lift the bottom scarf by the ends to form a link.

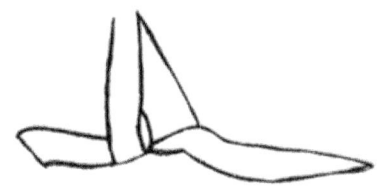

Place the link on top of your head, take the ends to the back and tie them together. Tuck in the ends on each side.

101 Ways To Tie A Scarf

6 FOREHEAD DRAPE

Place an oblong scarf around the back of your head. Bring the ends forward over your head and twist the ends twice.

Take the ends to the back again and tuck them in or tie a knot.

This idea also works well with a square scarf folded into a bias.

7 SMOOTH FOREHEAD DRAPE

To make the smooth forehead drape follow the instructions on the previous page except tie a smooth square knot instead of twisting the ends, then tuck the ends in neatly.

8 THE SIDE ROSETTE

Place an oblong scarf around your head. Take one panel under your hair and tie a knot at your ear.

Use two fingers as a guide to twist one panel into a rope and wind it around the knot. Twist the other panel into a rope and also wind it around the knot.

101 Ways To Tie A Scarf

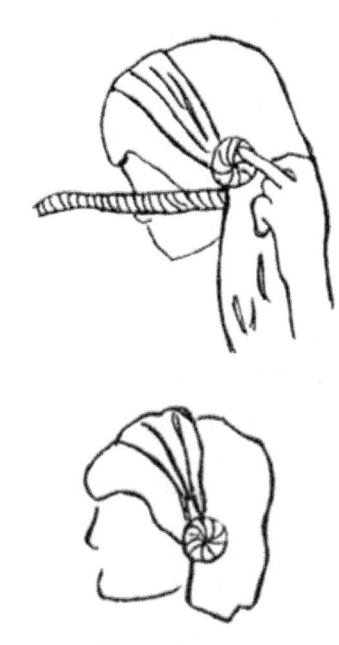

Secure the knot with a hairpin.

9 FULL COVERING SIDE ROSETTE

It is best to use a stretchy scarf to achieve the full covering side rosette. Spread the scarf over the head by separating the folds, then pull tightly toward the knot. Tuck the folds into the knot then secure carefully with hairpins.

10 THE HAIR WRAP

Fold a large square scarf into a bias until it is about four inches wide, then twist it into a rope. Place the rope around your forehead and tie a knot at the back.

Tuck your hair into the rope, one section at a time.

Bring the ends to the front and tie to finish the look or simply tuck them in.

11 CLASSY HAIR COVER

Fold a large square scarf in half in the form of a triangle. Place the folded edge of the scarf on your forehead and gather the side panels at the back in one hand.

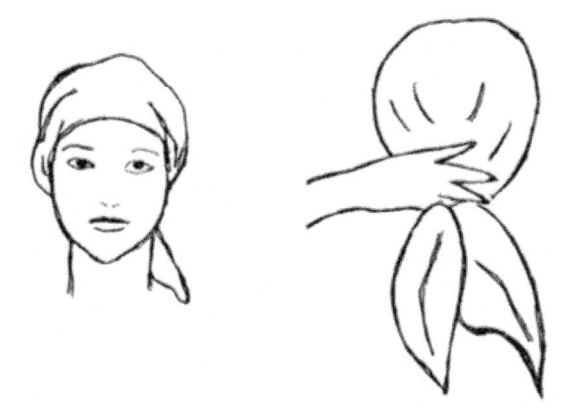

Secure the gathered scarf with a decorative ponytail holder.

Try a hat on top to finish the look!

12 EVERYDAY HAIR COVER

Fold a square scarf in half to form a triangle. Holding the opposite corners place the folded edge on your forehead.

Bring the two ends to the back and tie in a secure knot.

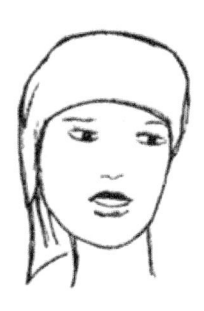

14 POOR WEATHER HIDEAWAY

Pick up the two corners of a straight edge on a large square scarf. Place the corners on the top of your head with the straight edge under your chin and tie a knot at the crown of your head.

Taking the side panels to the back of your head, tuck the scarf around your neck securely. Place a hat on top for a finished effect.

15 WINDY DAY COVER-UP

Place the straight edge of a large square scarf under your hair at the back of your head. Take the two ends of that edge to the top of your head and tie a square knot.

Tie a large square knot at the back of your head with the other two ends.

101 Ways To Tie A Scarf

This design makes an attractive cover-up for a windy day.

16 TRI-COLORED HAIR HOLDER

Take three different colored oblong chiffon, or other sheer fabric scarves and knot them together at one end. Twist them tightly and tie a knot in the other end.

Wrap the rope around your head and tie the end at the back of your neck, under your hair. If necessary, use hairpins to hold firmly in place.

17 STYLISH HAIR HOLDER

Place an oblong scarf on the top of your head and take the ends to the back of your neck.

Criss-cross the ends and take them back up to the top of your head and tie a knot.

Tuck the ends in on each side and, if necessary, fasten with a few hairpins.

18 NECK WRAPS

Scarves can be worn around the neck for any season – light fluttery scarves are best for spring and summer and your heavier wool or knit scarves are perfect for fall and winter!

19 ROPE TIE

Fold a small square scarf on the bias until it measures about three inches wide and then twist the scarf to form a rope.

Place the rope around your neck and tie a square knot.

20 CHOKER

For this effect use a medium square scarf. Follow the directions on the previous page, except wrap the rope around your neck twice.

21 NECKLACE

For this variation, use a longer square scarf, depending on how long you want your necklace to be.

22 BOW TIE

Fold a large square scarf in half into a rectangle. Keep folding in half until the scarf measures about three inches wide. Place the scarf around your neck and tie a simple overhand knot.

Now tie a second knot to form the square knot.

23 FLOWER TIE

For this variation, complete the bow tie on the previous page and ruffle the bow into a flower.

24 THE LOOSE ASCOT

Open a square scarf and place it on a flat surface. Pick up the center of the scarf and tie a simple overhand knot.

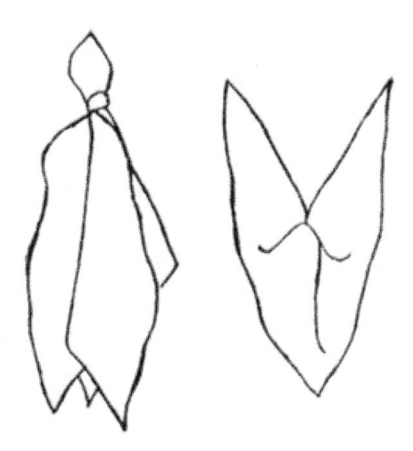

Holding opposite corners of the scarf, form a triangle with the knot hidden on the inside.

Place the scarf around your neck with the knot under your chin. Bring the ends forward under the panel and tie a secure knot. If the scarf is small, tie the knot at the back of the neck and tuck in the ends.

S. Denise Hoyle

25 THE ROMANTIC TWIST

Place a large square scarf on a flat surface. Pick up two corners of a straight edge with your fingers.

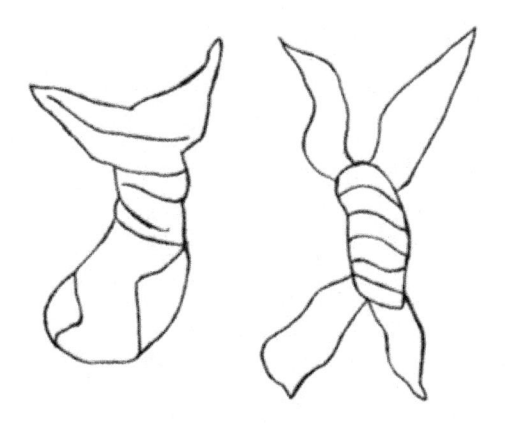

Twist the scarf in one direction. Be sure the first twist goes to the center of the scarf. Twist several times, keeping the twists fairly loose. Repeat with the other two ends.

Carefully pick up the twisted scarf and place it around your neck. Take the two ends and tie a square knot.

S. Denise Hoyle

26 THE WESTERN ASCOT

Fold a square scarf into a triangle and place the folded edge over your nose, then take the ends to the back of your head.

Criss-cross the panels at the back of your neck then bring them forward under your chin and tie a square knot. Tuck in the ends on each side.

Pull the scarf down and spread it over the knot.

27 UNFINISHED WESTERN ASCOT

Fold a very large square scarf into a triangle and place the fold under your chin, then continue as stated on the previous page.

28 FORMAL ASCOT

Drape an oblong scarf around your neck with one end hanging longer than the other.

Tie a loose square knot. Bring the longest panel up through the neck and spread the panel evenly over the knot.

101 Ways To Tie A Scarf

This ascot looks great with dressy blouses and suits!

29 FINISHED ASCOT

Fold an oblong scarf in thirds lengthwise and place the scarf in front of your neck then take the panels to the back. Criss-cross the panels at the back and carry them forward leaving one panel longer than the other.

Carry the longer panel over the short one and tie an overhand knot then smooth the panels.

101 Ways To Tie A Scarf

30 ROPE NECKLACE

Fold a square scarf on the bias to measure about three inches wide, then make a loose knot in the center. Next, make two more knots on each side of the center knot for a total of five knots.

Hang the scarf around your neck as you would a necklace then tie a square knot at the back of the neck.

31 NECK TWIST

Fold an oblong scarf in thirds lengthwise then fold the scarf in half the other way and place it around your neck. Open the loop and send the other two ends through it then slide the loop up by pulling the ends down.

Next, take both ends and twist them around the scarf on the side.

S. Denise Hoyle

32 ROPE TWIST

Hold one end of a large oblong scarf and twirl it with your wrist. Pick up the other end quickly once twisted.

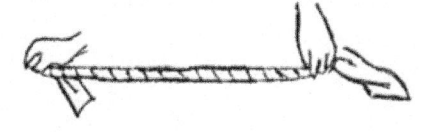

Place both ends in one hand and let scarf wind itself up.

Drape the twisted scarf around your neck and put the two ends through the loop you've created.

S. Denise Hoyle

33 NECK TIE

Drape an oblong scarf around your neck keeping one end longer than the other, then tie a loose overhand knot in the long panel.

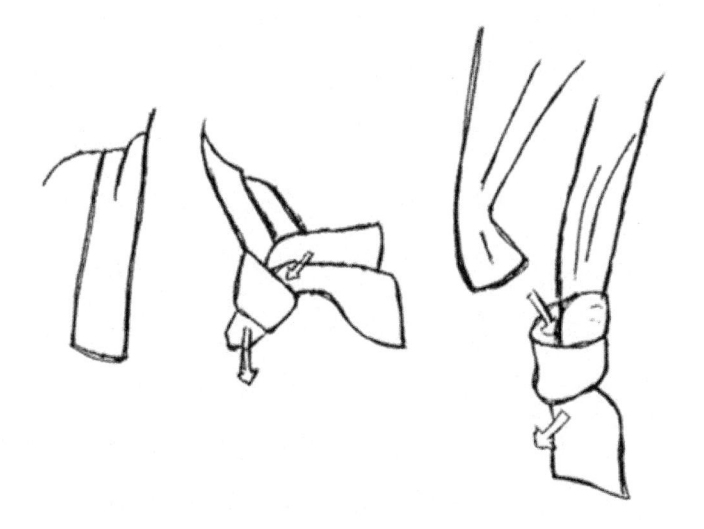

Send the short panel down through the loop of the knot and position the knot to your liking.

S. Denise Hoyle

34 CASUAL ROPE

Place an oblong scarf around your neck and tie an overhand knot. Wind each panel around the neck area of scarf and secure the ends within the twists.

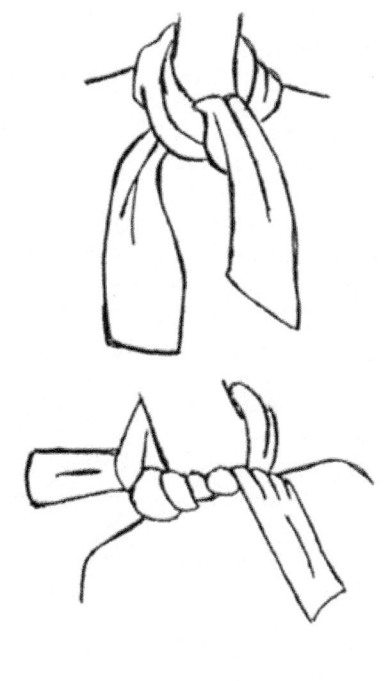

S. Denise Hoyle

35 NECK ROSETTE

Place a scarf that has been folded in half on the bias around your neck and send both ends down through the loop you have formed.

Next, tie the ends of the scarf together, twist the panels then wrap the twisted scarf around the looped area.

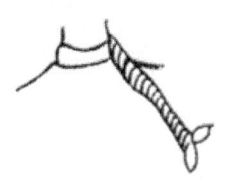

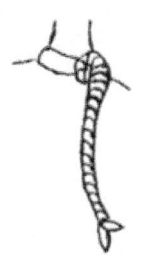

S. Denise Hoyle

36 LOOSE NECK BOW

Place an oblong scarf around your neck and form a loop with one panel.

Tie a simple knot around the loop with the other panel.

S. Denise Hoyle

37 SHOULDER WRAP

Fold an oblong scarf in half lengthwise. Lift the scarf by holding the opposite diagonal corners, thus shaping two triangles.

Place the folded edge around your neck and tie a square knot.

S. Denise Hoyle

38 SIDE WRAP

Follow the instructions on the previous page except wear your scarf off to the side.

39 COLLAR DRESSER

Drape an oblong scarf around your neck, keeping one end longer, and tie a square knot.

Bring the long panel up through the neck and spread it evenly over the knot.

Pick up the middle of the long panel, wrap it around the first button and send button and scarf through the buttonhole. Continue this procedure for each button.

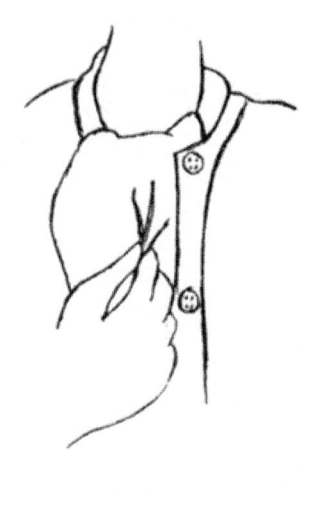

101 Ways To Tie A Scarf

40 NECK WRAP KNOT

Tie a single knot in the center of an oblong scarf.

Center the knot at the front of your neck and take the panels to the back. Criss-cross the panels and carry them forward pulling the ends through the knot, then tighten.

101 Ways To Tie A Scarf

41 PLEATED FLOWER WRAP

Place an oblong scarf around your neck and, keeping one panel longer than the other as shown, tie an overhand knot. Pleat the longer panel from the bottom up to the knot.

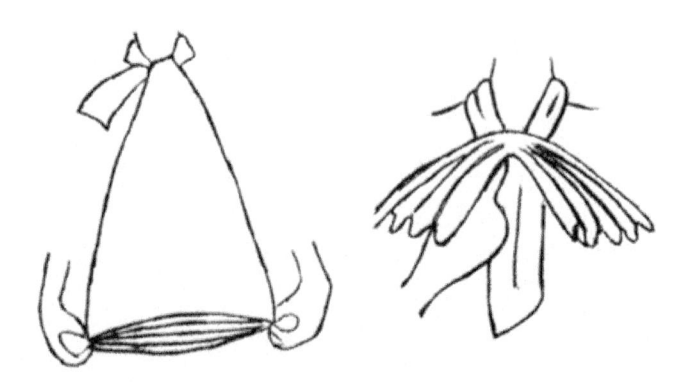

Wrap the short panel around the pleated one, insert it through the loop you've formed then pull to tighten.

101 Ways To Tie A Scarf

42 CASUAL PLEATED FLOWER

Follow the design on the previous page, except use a bias scarf and tie the knot at a lower position.

43 PUFFED NECK WRAP

Place an oblong scarf around your neck and, leaving one panel slightly longer than the other as shown, tie a square knot.

Pull some of the longer panel up behind the knot to form the puff and lay over the knot.

Spread and arrange the puff as desired.

44 LOOPED NECK WRAP

Tie a loose knot about five inches from one end of an oblong scarf. Form a loop near the knot with the longer panel and feed it up through the knot.

Keep making loops to form a chain. Leave about six inches for finishing. Take the end up through the last loop to secure your chain.

S. Denise Hoyle

45 PLEATED NECK WRAP

Starting about ten inches from one end of a bias scarf, pleat it with your fingertips to about the same distance from the other end.

Hold the pleats in one hand and stretch a rubber band over the pleats. Roll the rubber band to the center of the scarf. Now hold the pleats so the rubber band isn't visible as it forms a ruffle.

S. Denise Hoyle

46 THE SQUARE KNOT

Place a scarf around your neck leaving one end longer (2) than the other. Cross panel (2) over (1) and send it up through the neck.

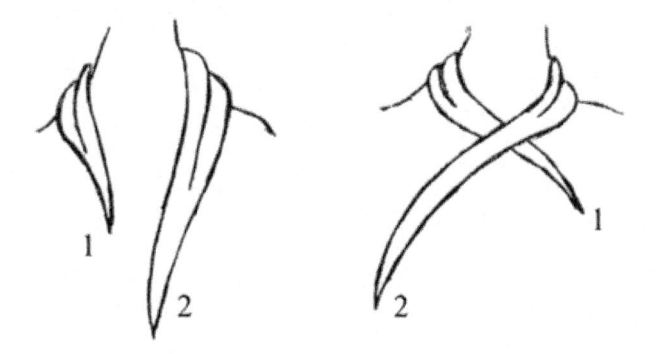

Cross panel (2) over panel (1) below the first part of the knot and bring (2) through the little opening.

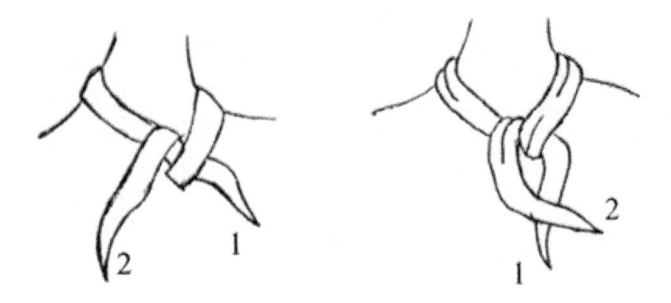

Tighten the knot and spread the panels to make your square knot.

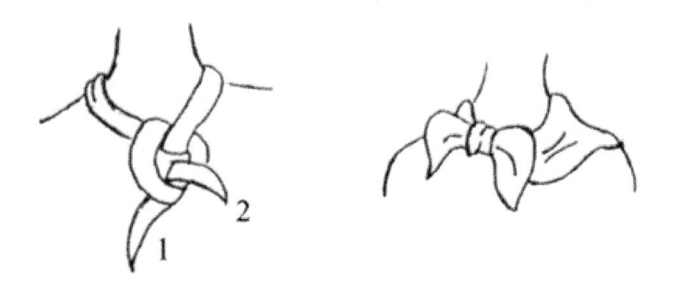

47 TAILORED NECK TIE

Drape an oblong scarf or tie around your neck, keeping one end (2) slightly longer than the other (1). Carry panel (2) over panel (1), then under, then over again.

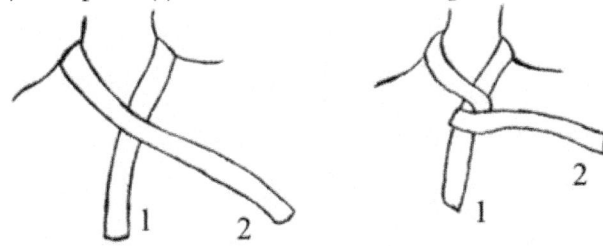

Take Panel (2) up through the neck area then send it down the front through the loop you've formed.

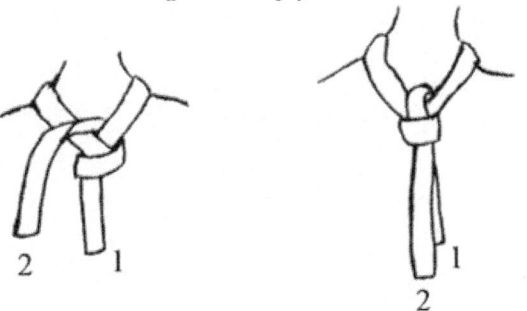

48 THE WINDSOR KNOT

Follow the step by step illustrations below to complete the Windsor knot.

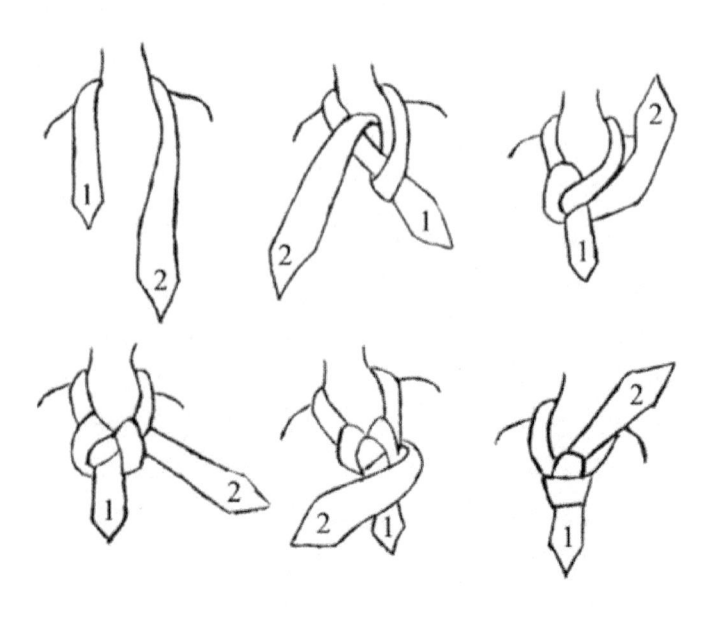

101 Ways To Tie A Scarf

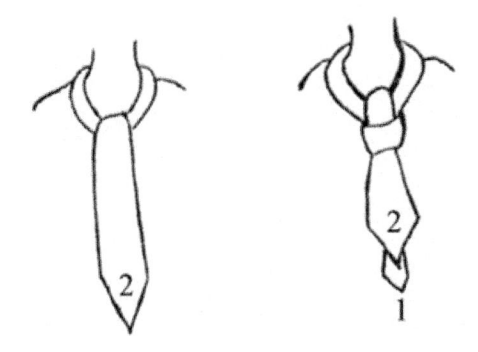

49 TRADITIONAL BOW TIE

Follow the step by step illustrations below to tie the traditional bow tie.

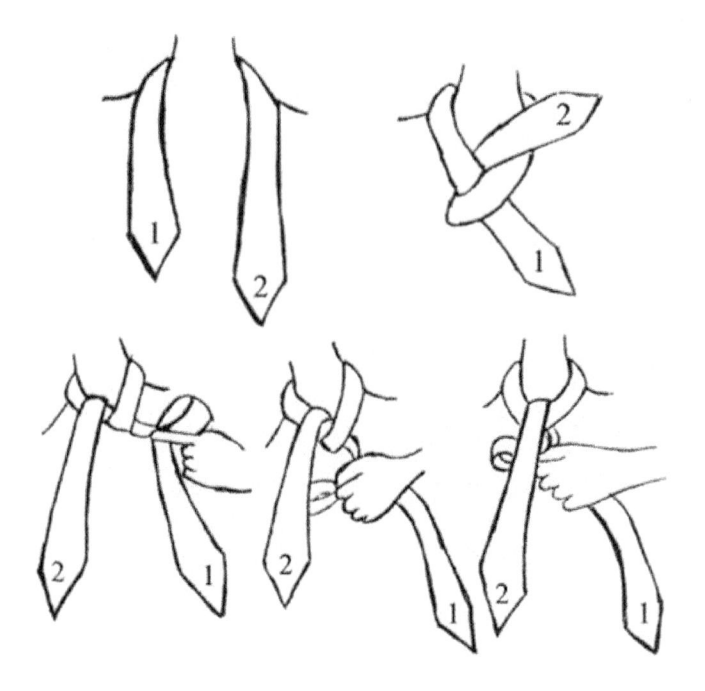

101 Ways To Tie A Scarf

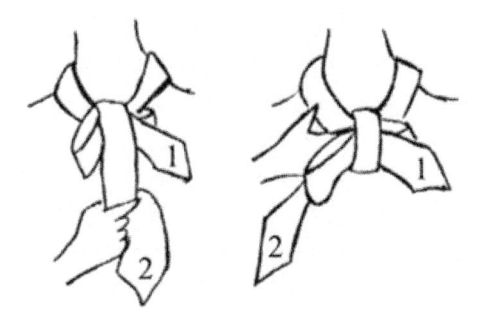

50 BASIC BOWS

Following are just a few basic bows you can use to dress up a blouse or use with a suit.

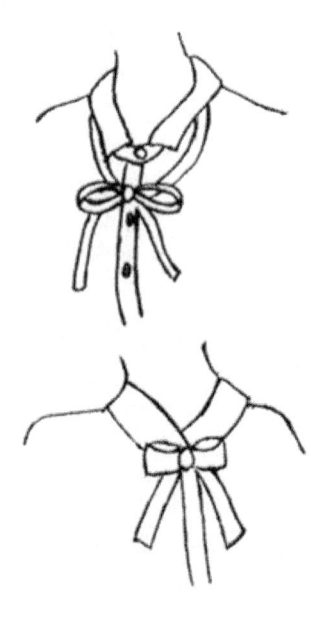

101 Ways To Tie A Scarf

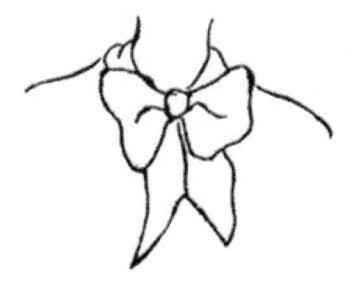

51 USING A BUCKLE

Drape a scarf around your neck and feed the ends of the scarf through the openings of the buckle one at a time.

52 WAIST WRAPS

Wrap a scarf around your waist instead of a belt for a whole new look! You can use scarves around the waist to hide "trouble" spots or to highlight your best attributes!

53 BRAIDED WAIST WRAP

Tie three oblong scarves together at one end and braid, then tie them together at the other end. Tie the band around your waist. Hint: if the scarves are too bulky to knot the ends before tying, try using colorful rubber bands.

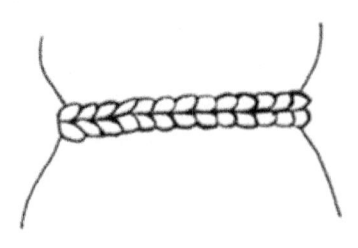

54 SASH

Fold a large square scarf until it is about ten inches wide. Twist the scarf loosely then wrap around your waist, tie a knot then tuck in the ends.

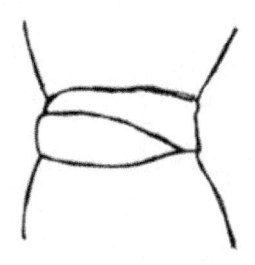

55 KNOTTED WAIST WRAP

In the middle of an oblong scarf, tie a loose knot. Place the scarf around your waist with the knot in the middle, then tie a knot at the back and tuck in the ends.

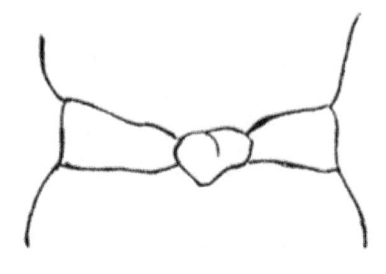

56 FLOWERED WAIST WRAP

Place an oblong scarf around your waist and tie a square knot. Twist the ends together and wrap them around the knot to form a rose. Tuck the ends into the center of the rose to finish the look.

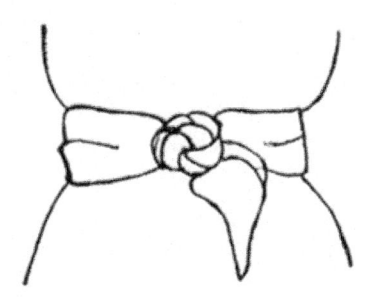

57 LOOPED WAIST WRAP

Tie a loose knot about five inches from one end of an oblong scarf. Form a loop near the knot with the longer panel and feed it up through the knot.

Keep making loops to form a chain. Leave about six inches for finishing. Take the end up through the last loop to secure your chain.

101 Ways To Tie A Scarf

58 TOPS & SKIRTS

Did you know that you can even tie your larger scarves in ways that they can be worn as tops or even skirts? Check out these fun wraps!

59 HIP WRAP & BANDEAU

Twist a long oblong scarf in the middle, place it around your bust and tie a knot in the back. Fold a large square scarf in half into a triangle, drape it around your hips and tie a knot at the side.

101 Ways To Tie A Scarf

60 HALTER TOP

Place two matching or complementary colored scarves on a table side by side and tie a knot with the two inner corners. Fold the bottom corners to the top. Pick up the scarves and place the knot in the center of your chest. Tie the outer corners at your waist and the top corners behind your neck.

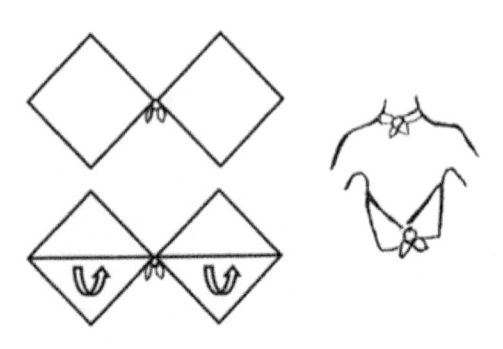

101 Ways To Tie A Scarf

61 BLOUSON

Tie a knot with the two corners of a large square scarf behind your neck. Tie a knot with the other two ends behind your waist. Finish the look with a belt or another scarf at the waist. This style looks terrific under a structured blazer!

101 Ways To Tie A Scarf

62 CRISS-CROSS HALTER

Tie a square knot at one end of two bias ties, place the knot in the center of your chest, wrap the scarves around your chest, criss-cross them at the back, bring the ends under your arms to the front, take the ends behind your neck and tie a knot.

63 SLASHED BIKINI TOP

Tie an oblong scarf around your bust. Feed a second oblong scarf through the first one in the center of your chest and tie a knot behind your neck.

64 BODICE

Fold a large square scarf in half into a triangle and place it diagonally across your chest. Take one end under your arm and the other end over the opposite shoulder, cross the ends under your arm and tie a knot on top of your shoulder.

101 Ways To Tie A Scarf

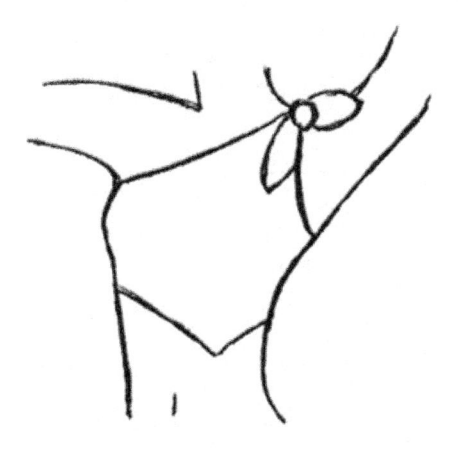

65 BIKINI TOP & SKIRT

To make the top, tie a loose knot in the center of an oblong scarf, place it around your bust and tie a square knot at the back.

For the skirt, place a large square scarf around your waist or hip, form a point with the ends, then tie and tuck them inside the skirt to finish the look.

101 Ways To Tie A Scarf

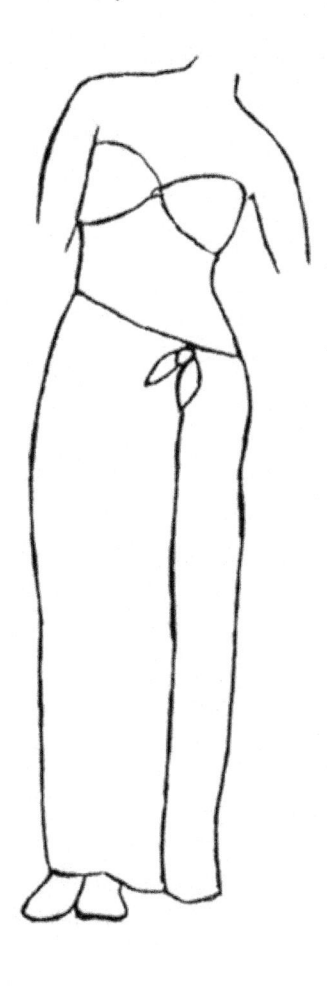

66 SHAWLS

Shawls are a great addition to any wardrobe and can worn in several different ways!

67 DRAPED SHAWL

Fold a large square shawl in half into a triangle, drape the shawl over your shoulder and secure either the front or both ends with a belt. This design works well with any outfit!

101 Ways To Tie A Scarf

68 FOLDED SHAWL

Fold a large square shawl in half into a rectangle and keep folding in half until it measures approximately ten inches wide. Place the shawl over one shoulder and secure it with a belt at your waist.

101 Ways To Tie A Scarf

69 KNOTTED SHAWL

Fold a large square shawl in half into a triangle, place it across your shoulders and take the panels to the back.

Tie a square knot in the panels at the back to secure your shawl.

101 Ways To Tie A Scarf

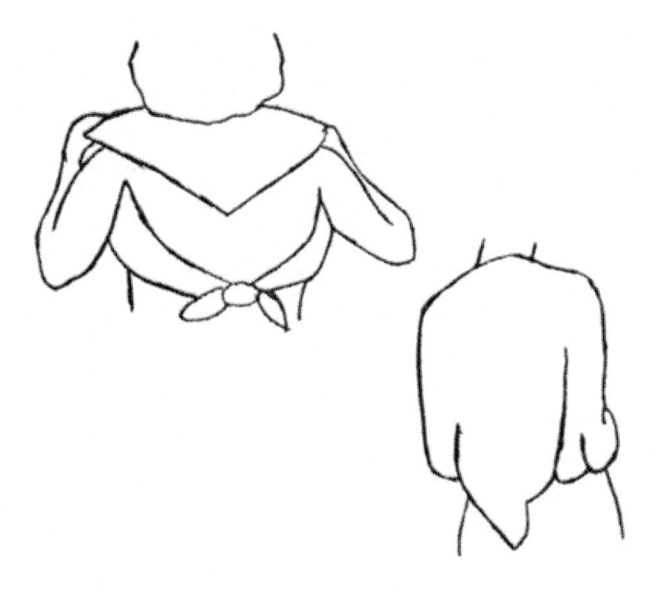

70 HAT WRAPS

Scarves are a fabulous way to change the look of your favorite hats! Simply add a matching or contrasting scarf using one of these wrap methods and you can make a hat work with any outfit

71 RUFFLED HAT WRAP

Pleat a medium square scarf with your fingers and wrap it around your hat. Pull the ends through a scarf clip, spread the ruffle and close the clip.

72 ROPED HAT WRAP

Twist a square scarf into a rope, wrap it around your hat, tie a knot and spread the ends.

73 BOWED HAT WRAP

Wrap a scarf around your hat and make a bow at the back.

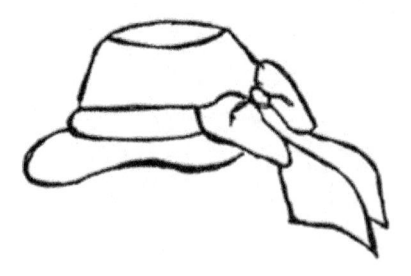

74 PLEATED HAT WRAP

Pleat an oblong or medium scarf until it measures about three inches wide. Place it around your hat and tie a square knot or pin in place for added security.

75 USING A SCARF CLIP

Scarf clips are available on eBay, Amazon, Etsy and at your favorite local accessory store and you'll be amazed at how a scarf clip can not only change the whole look of your scarf but can also add stability.

76 HEAD WRAP

Fold two square scarves until they measure about four inches wide each. Form a cross by placing one on top of the other at an angle.

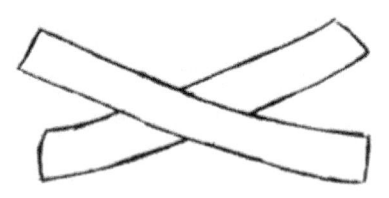

Pick up the bottom scarf by the ends to form a link. Place the link on top of your head, take one panel behind your head, take the ends of the scarf down through the scarf clip, spread the panels and close the clip.

101 Ways To Tie A Scarf

77 FULL HEAD WRAP

Follow the directions on the previous page then after placing the link on top of your head, bring the panels to the back of your head. Send the ends through the clip and close the clip. Spread the panels to cover your hair.

101 Ways To Tie A Scarf

78 PIRATE'S CAP

Fold a medium square scarf in half into a triangle and place it on top of your head with the folded edge in front. Hold both panels in one hand on one side of your head, bring the back panel forward and put all three ends through the scarf clip. Slide the clip up to tighten, close the clip and spread the panels.

79 BONNET

Fold a large square scarf in half into a rectangle and place the outer edges against your neck. Send all four corners down through the clip, slide the clip up about five inches and close it.

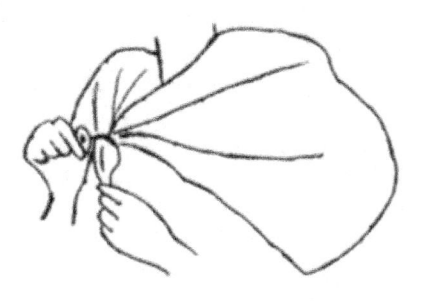

Bring the folded panel up from the back to the top of your head and tuck the leading edges under. Open the clip and pull on the ends of the scarf until it fits snugly.

S. Denise Hoyle

80 BOW TIE HEAD WRAP

Fold a square scarf in half into a triangle and place the folded edge along your forehead.

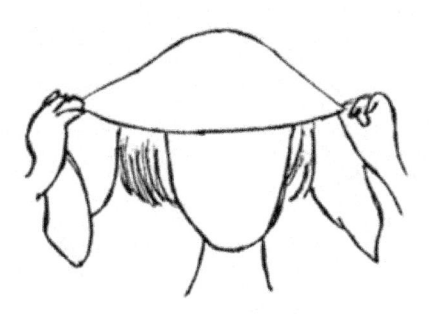

Take the panels to the back of your head and hold them in one hand. Hold the ends close to the nape of your neck and push that part through the scarf clip. Spread the folds to form a bow and close the clip.

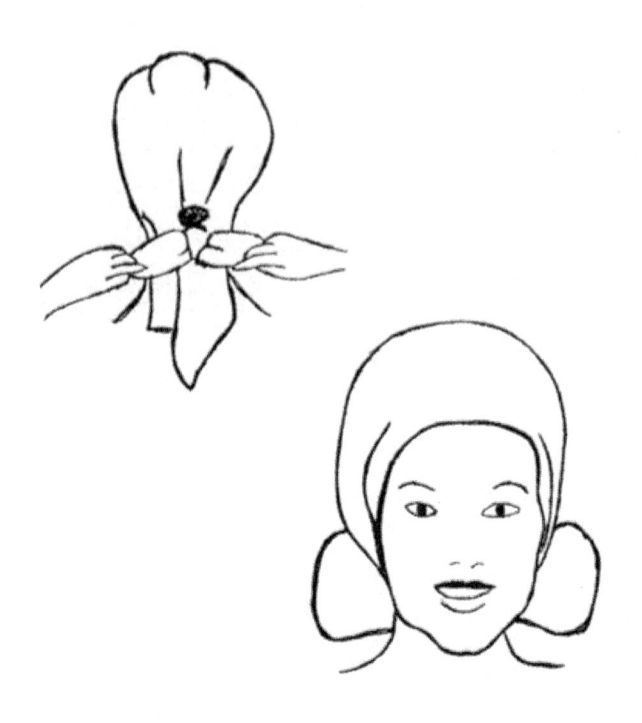

81 RUFFLED FLOWER

Pleat a straight edge of a large square scarf and hold the pleated end in one hand while sliding your hand down the scarf to gather the other end.

Place the scarf around your head. Take both ends to one side holding both pleated ends in one hand and send them through the clip. Close the clip and spread the pleats to look like a ruffled flower.

82 BOWED HEAD WRAP

Place an oblong scarf over the top of your head and take both panels to the side of your head. Pinch the edges of the scarf and send them through the scarf clip. Separate the folds to form a bow and close the clip.

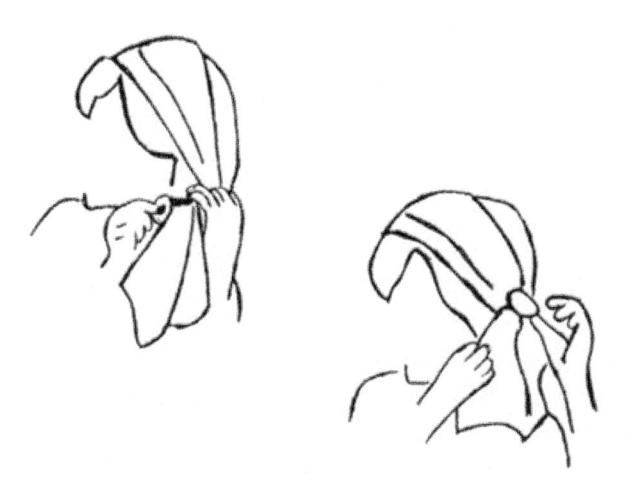

S. Denise Hoyle

83 LOOSE HAIR COVER

Fold a large oblong scarf in half lengthwise and place the folded edge around your neck. Send the ends through the scarf clip and close the clip about five inches from the end of the scarf.

Spread the scarf around your neck into a single layer and cover your head with it. Tuck the edges under. Open the clip and pull on the ends until it fits snugly then close it again.

S. Denise Hoyle

84 KNOTTED HEAD WRAP

Tie a loose knot in the center of a long narrow scarf. Place the knot on top of your head and take both panels to the side of your head.

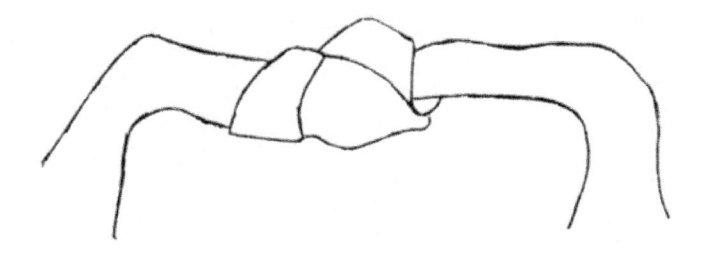

Pass the ends of the scarf through the scarf clip, slide the clip up and close it.

S. Denise Hoyle

85 NECK WRAP

Fold a square scarf until it measures about four inches wide. Place the scarf around your neck keeping the ends even and send both ends through the scarf clip.

Spread the panels to each side to finish the look.

S. Denise Hoyle

86 CHOKER

Roll a medium square scarf until it measures about three inches wide. Place the scarf around your neck and send the ends through the scarf clip.

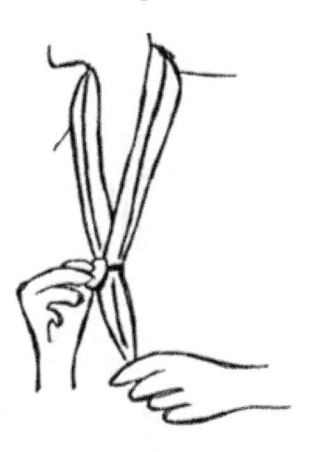

Slide the clip up to your neck and close it. Take an end to the back of your neck on each side and tuck in the ends.

87 HALF BOW

Fold a small square scarf in half into a triangle. Place the folded edge around your neck keeping the ends even then send the ends through the scarf clip.

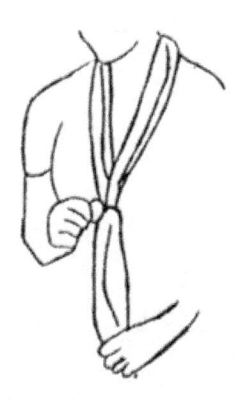

Slide the clip up to your neck, cross the panels below the clip and send one end of the scarf back down through the clip about an inch. Spread the bow and close the clip.

88 NECK BOW

Follow the instructions on the previous page then send the second end through the clip about an inch. Spread the sides and close the clip.

89 MULTI-COLORED NECK BOW

Knot two scarves together at one end and drape them around your neck with the knot at the back. Wrap the scarves around your neck as many times as you can, leaving the ends about six inches long.

Send the ends of the scarf through the scarf clip. Slide the clip up to your neck and close it.

101 Ways To Tie A Scarf

90 RUFFLED NECK BOW

Pleat one edge of a small scarf. Hold the pleats in one hand and run your other hand down the scarf to pleat the entire length of the scarf.

Place the scarf around your neck and fee both ends through the scarf clip.

101 Ways To Tie A Scarf

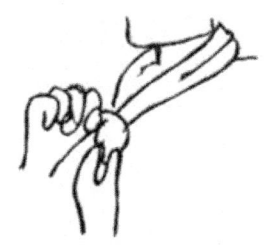

Spread the scarf ends and close the clip.

91 TRIANGULAR NECK WRAP

Fold a small square scarf in half into a triangle shape. Place the folded edge around your neck keeping one end longer and send both ends through the scarf clip.

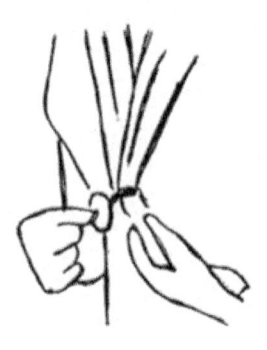

Slide the clip up to your neck. Spread the longest panel then spread the short panel directly on top of it and close the clip.

101 Ways To Tie A Scarf

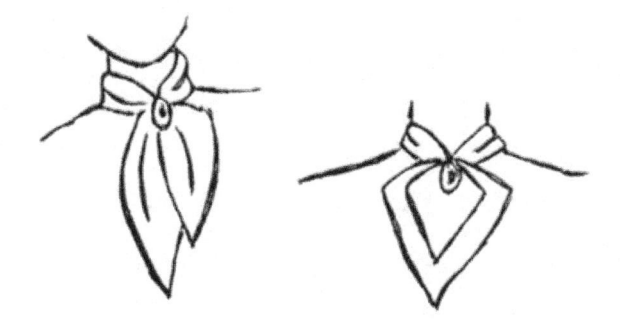

92 DOUBLE NECK PANEL

Complete the design on the previous page using an open-faced scarf clip. Open the clip, take the bottom panel back up through the neck and then down through the open face of your scarf clip. Spread the panel and close the clip.

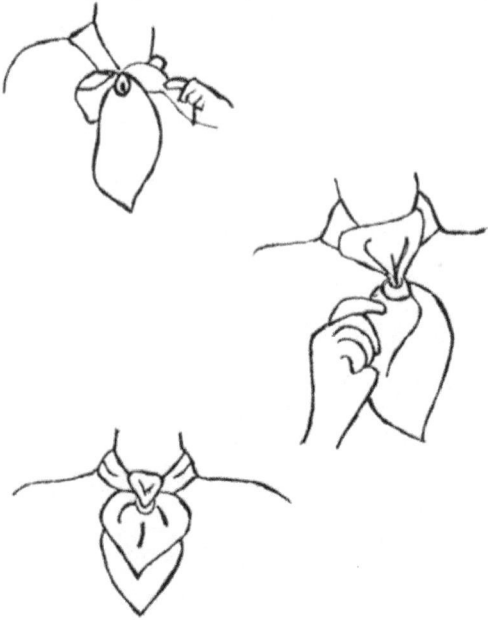

93 SHOULDER BOW

Tie a knot in the ends of two different colored scarves and place them around your shoulders with the knot at the back of your neck. Fold the scarves into two triangles, pinch the center of the folded edges together and send them through the scarf clip. Pull the folds through to form a bow and close the clip.

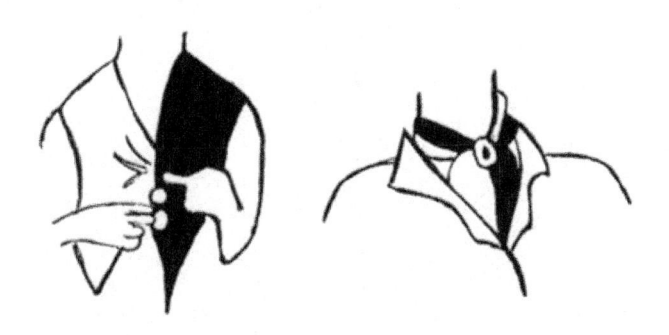

94 CLIPPED ASCOT

Fold a square scarf in half into a triangle. Place the folded edge around your neck keeping the ends even and send the ends through the scarf clip. Slide the clip up to your neck.

Take a panel to the side – spread the other panel. Bring the side panel back and spread it over the first one and close the clip. Take the bottom panel up through the neck and spread it over the clip.

101 Ways To Tie A Scarf

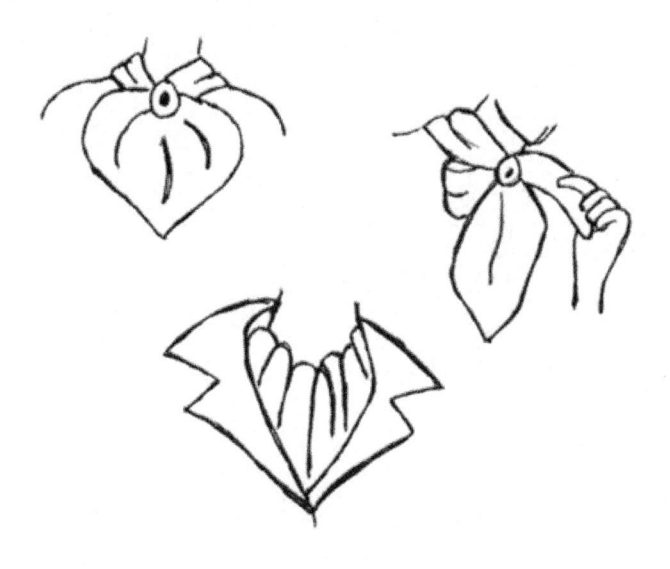

95 PUFFED ASCOT

Fold a square scarf in half into a triangle. Place the folded edge around your neck keeping the ends even and tie a square knot with the ends.

Turn the knot so it rests at the back of your neck. Pinch the folded edge that is now under your chin and pull it through the scarf clip to make a puff. Spread the puff and close the clip.

101 Ways To Tie A Scarf

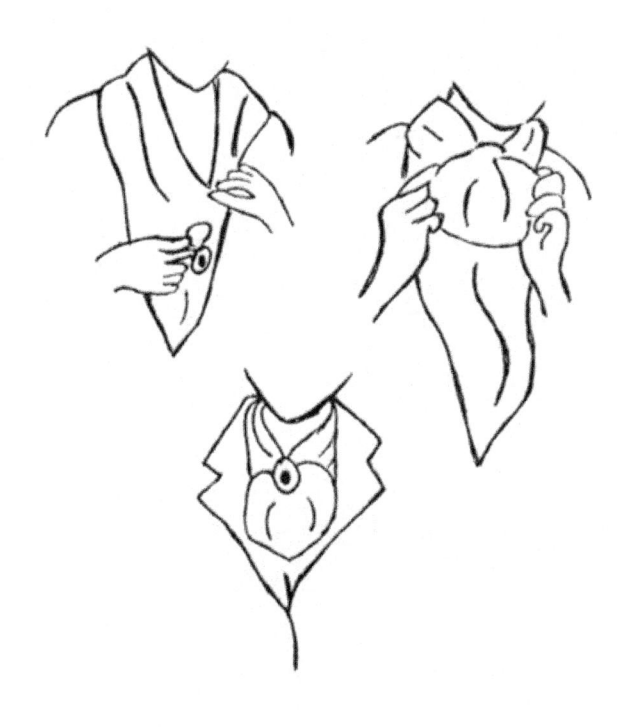

96 PUFFED JABOT

Follow the instructions on the previous page. Open the clip and continue to pull the scarf through until there is just a little bit left.

Tuck what's left into the back of the puff and form a pocket with the puff then close the clip.

101 Ways To Tie A Scarf

97 BOWED ASCOT

Fold a medium square scarf in half into a triangle. Place the triangle at the front of your neck and take the two ends to the back.

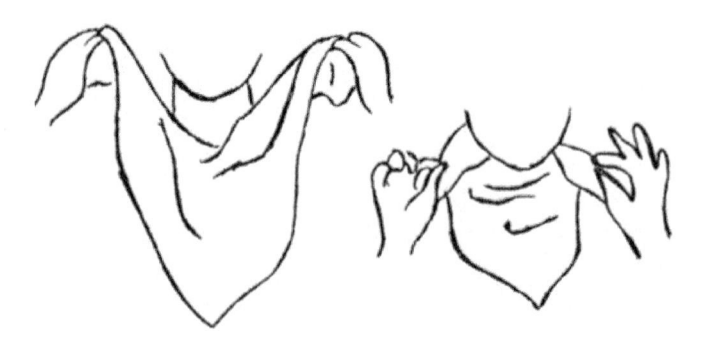

Cross the ends at the back then bring them to the front and send them down through the scarf clip. Slide the clip up to the desired spot.

101 Ways To Tie A Scarf

Spread the ends out and close the clip.

98 CLIPPED COLLAR

Fold a square scarf in half into a rectangle. Pick up two opposite corners to form two triangles.

Place the long end around your neck keeping the ends even then send the ends through the scarf clip. Slide the clip up about five inches then close it. Spread each panel.

101 Ways To Tie A Scarf

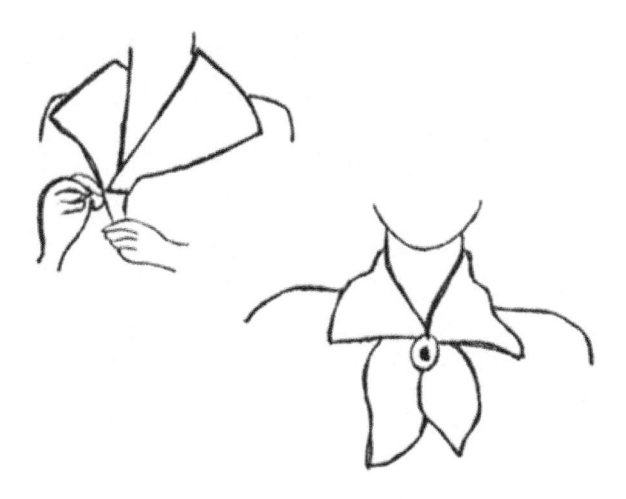

99 PUFFY COLLAR

Follow the instructions on the previous page. Open the clip and slide it all the way up to your neck. Spread the panels as shown and close the clip.

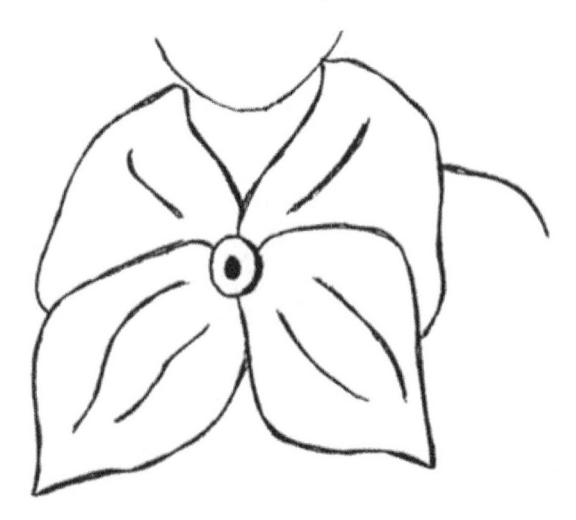

100 RUFFLED COLLAR

Fold a square scarf in half into a triangle and place it around your shoulders.

Pick up the top panel of the outside edges and pinch them together at the center then send the pinched edges down through the scarf clip.

Separate the edges and pull the puffs to form a bow then close the clip.

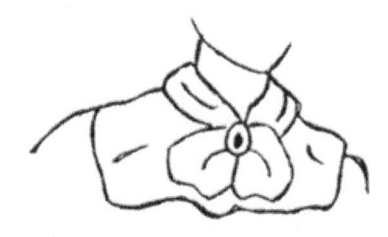

101 BOWED COLLAR

Fold a large square scarf in half into a triangle and place the folded edge around your neck, keeping the ends even. Pinch the center of the folded edges together and push them through the scarf clip about three inches.

Separate the fold and pull to make a bow then close the clip.

S. Denise Hoyle

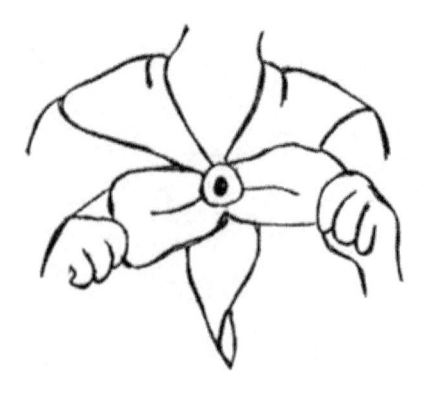

102 FLOWERED COLLAR

Follow the instructions on the previous page using an open-faced clip. Open the clip and make the bow as big as possible. Take the upper edges of the bow and send them through the open face of the clip. Keep pulling them through to form the petals.

When the petals are arranged as you like them, close the clip.

S. Denise Hoyle

103 PUFFED FLOWER

Fold a square scarf in half into a triangle and place it around your shoulders. Pick up the outside edges of the scarf and hold them in the center in one hand.

Feed the edges down through the scarf clip.

Separate the edges and pull to form four petals.

104 SIDE CLIPPED WRAP

Pin your scarf clip with a safety pin on the underside of your garment to create a bar. Fold a medium square scarf in half into a triangle and place it around your neck. Feed one panel through each half of your scarf clip loop.

Spread the panels and close the clip.

105 FULL NECK WRAP

Fold a medium square scarf in half into a rectangle and place the scarf around your neck with the outside edges next to it. Send the four corners through the scarf clip and slide it up close to your neck.

Spread the panels and close the clip.

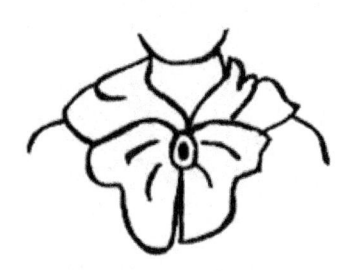

106 CLASSY NECK WRAP

Fold a medium square scarf in half lengthwise and keep folding until it measures about five inches wide. Place the scarf around your neck and feed the ends through your scarf clip. Keeping the ends even spread them and close the clip.

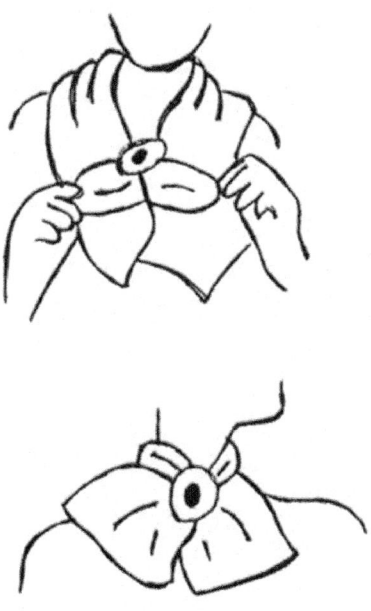

107 CLIPPED ROMANTIC TWIST

Pick up two corners of a large square scarf and begin to twist in one direction keeping the twists fairly loose.

Place the scarf around your neck while holding both ends in one hand. Feed the ends through the scarf clip, adjust as desired and close the clip.

101 Ways To Tie A Scarf

108 HEIGHTENING NECK WRAP

Fold an oblong scarf in thirds lengthwise until it measures about five inches wide. Place the scarf in front of your neck. Take the ends to the back, criss-cross the panels and bring them back to the front.

Feed the ends of the scarf down through the scarf clip.

101 Ways To Tie A Scarf

Push the scarf clip up to your neck. Pull one panel to the back and close the clip.

109 CONCLUSION

Keep in mind that the art of scarf making and tying depends mostly on the imagination, something we were all born with. So use your imagination and you'll never run out of creative new twists to enhance your wardrobe and your figure!

110 RESOURCES

http://SewWithSarah.com ~ Your pattern and pattern making headquarters!

http://PlusSizeChildren.com ~ Patterns, classes, books and links that make it easier to sew for plus size children!

http://PatternsThatFitYou.com ~ The online fashion design school teaches the art of custom fitting patterns and pattern making to beginners and experts alike.

http://Patterns2Go.com ~ A variety of patterns to choose from – sewing, crafting, knitting, crochet, tatting, and more.

http://SewMachineRepair.com ~ Learn how to repair your own treadle, serger and sewing machines and save yourself time, money and frustration.

http://CouponClutch.com ~ Carry your coupons in one of these fashionable fabric covered 3 ring binders.

http://ShopperStrategy.com ~ Be a better shopper!

http://SewingBusiness.com ~ Information plus tutorials for those who sew and for those in the business of sewing for others.

Printed in Great Britain
by Amazon